The I L♥ve Mysteries Fun Book

How to Be a Super Sleuth

by Dr. Lynda Madison

Illustrated by Lauren Scheuer

★ American Girl®

Published by American Girl Publishing, Inc.

Copyright © 2006 by American Girl, LLC

Questions or comments? Call 1-800-845-0005, visit our Web site at **americangirl.com**, or write to Customer Service, American Girl, 8400 Fairway Place, Middleton, WI 53562-0497.

Printed in China
09 10 11 12 13 14 15 LEO 11 10 9 8 7 6 5 4

Dr. Lynda Madison is a licensed psychologist and director of behavioral health services at Children's Hospital, Omaha. She is a nationally recognized speaker on the topic of adolescent girls.

Editorial Development: Therese Kauchak Maring

Art Direction & Design: Chris Lorette David

Production: Kendra Schluter, Mindy Rappe, Jeannette Bailey, Judith Lary

Illustrations: Lauren Scheuer

Dear Reader,

Did you ever think you'd make a great detective, or secret agent, or scientist? Do you like finding clues, breaking codes, and solving mysteries that you find in everyday life?

This collection of quizzes and other fun paper-and-pencil activities is made especially for fact-finding girls with inquiring minds— like you!

Your friends at American Girl

Contents

Your Sleuth Style

The world is full of lots of mysteries, and it takes different kinds of people to solve them all.

Some people investigate crimes, and others like figuring out how things work. Still others are curious about what makes people act the way they do.

Find out your sleuth style!

5

What kind of super sleuth are you?

Your everyday behavior can give you hints about what kind of super sleuth you might like to be. Check off the statements below that describe something you would do.

☐ **1.** You arrive home from a long day at school and search for a quiet corner where you can read a book.

☐ **2.** Your friends plan a sleepover in a tent and invite you to come along. You run home quickly to pack your bag.

☐ **3.** Your sister screams that there's a spider in her room, so you rush in and catch it in a jar. You watch it for a few minutes to see how it walks and eats.

☐ **4.** You've been waiting in the doctor's office a l-o-o-o-ng time. You entertain yourself by reading an encyclopedia you find on a shelf.

☐ **5.** A dog is loose in your neighborhood. You chase it through back-yards and alleys, running so fast that you're out of breath when you catch it.

☐ **6.** You have one space left to fill on your school schedule, and you must choose between science and literature. You sign up for science.

☐ **7.** When you read the newspaper, you don't grab the comics first. You search the headlines for the latest interesting scientific discovery.

☐ **8.** You and your friends have nothing to do one afternoon. You take over the kitchen and mix ingredients to see if you can create a new cookie.

☐ **9.** It's Saturday night and you have nothing to do. You look for a TV detective show that has a good police chase.

☐ **10.** You read books or magazines on just about any subject.

☐ **11.** Your friends run to tell you that they think they found a buried treasure under a rock. You grab a shovel so you can dig right in.

☐ **12.** You find an old radio that someone threw out. You know where the tools are and have lots of time, so you take it apart to see how it works.

☐ **13.** Your family disagrees about the name of a flower, with everyone claiming it's something different. You look it up in your plant book.

Turn the page to find the answer key.

Scoring
Super Sleuth

If your answers were mostly red, you could be a

Senior Scientist.

You enjoy looking at scientific details and don't mind getting your hands dirty for the sake of a project. You might enjoy solving a crime by working in a lab, checking out DNA and fingerprints to see if they match the suspect's.

If your answers were mostly green, you could be an

Information Specialist.

You love knowing all the facts or searching them out when you don't. You might enjoy solving crimes by doing research in books or newspapers to see what has been discovered in the past, or by searching the Internet for information about the details of the crime.

If your answers were mostly blue, you could be a

Crime-Scene Investigator.

You like the people-to-people interaction as well as the chase. You might enjoy being a policewoman or private eye, tracking down suspects and arresting criminals.

S.P.I.E.S.—
fact or fiction?

There are all kinds of "S.P.I.E.S." out there—Scientists, Police, Investigators, Experimenters, and Special Agents. What do you know about the experts? Decide whether each statement is a **fact** (true) or fiction (false).

Fact Fiction

☐ ☐ **1.** None of these people had to go to college.

☐ ☐ **2.** A special agent might watch and arrest criminals.

☐ ☐ **3.** All people who do experiments were at the very top of their class in high school.

☐ ☐ **4.** Most scientists love to learn new things, do experiments, and explore nature's secrets.

☐ ☐ **5.** All scientists have the same personality.

☐ ☐ **6.** Some scientists have jobs in zoos, schools, museums, and aquariums.

☐ ☐ **7.** An experimenter, like an experimental psychologist, could try to figure out how the eye sends messages to the brain.

☐ ☐ **8.** A police detective does investigations to prevent crimes or solve criminal cases.

☐ ☐ **9.** A lie-detector test could be done by a police detective.

☐ ☐ **10.** An investigator might secretly watch someone in order to catch him or her in illegal activity.

Turn the page to find the answers.

Scoring
S.P.I.E.S.

1. **Fiction:** For most of these fields, a college degree is required.

2. **Fact:** Some special agents, like those in the FBI, do chase down criminals.

3. **Fiction:** Some very successful scientists were not first in their class. Doing well in school is important, but so are curiosity and interest.

4. **Fact:** Science is all about finding the answers to puzzling questions.

5. **Fiction:** All scientists are different. Some are outgoing and others are shy. Some are serious and others tell jokes. You can find all sorts of personalities among people who do the same job.

6. **Fact:** Scientists are employed in many different areas, working on problems faced by people, plants, or animals in those environments.

7. **Fact:** This kind of scientific study could be done by a biologist, a psychologist, or a neuroscientist.

8. **Fact:** A police detective might interview suspects or look up information on a computer, all to try to solve a case.

9. **Fact:** Some police are specially trained to use lie-detector tests to help solve crimes.

10. **Fact:** Investigators sometimes go "under cover" to figure out what someone is doing.

Mission: Discover your sleuth skills

Do you have skills that might come in handy for solving mysteries? Choose the answer that best describes what you'd do in each situation.

1. Your family is renting a cabin for the weekend and the electricity goes out because of a storm. With no computer or television, you would . . .

   a. read a book.

   b. do a jigsaw puzzle.

   c. make up stories about people you saw at the camp store earlier today.

2. You're at summer camp and the counselors are judging a contest. You're most likely to win the title of . . .

   a. Super Smarty. You looked up the names of all the native trees and bugs and taught them to everyone else.

   b. Perfect Packer. You figured out how to fit more into your suitcase than any other camper did.

   c. Best Actor. You weren't afraid to get up onstage and talk in front of other people during the camp play.

3. You have a couple of days off from school because the teachers are at a conference. You're most likely to . . .

   a. watch the news or read a newspaper.

   b. work on a project, like building a birdhouse or decorating a cake.

   c. e-mail a friend or talk to her on the phone.

4. You're working on a homework assignment and can't figure out the answer. You are most likely to . . .

   a. reread the chapter or look up the info on the Internet.

   b. decide to organize your desk or bookshelf.

   c. ask around to find someone who might have the answer.

Turn the page to find your sleuth skills.

Scoring

Mission: Discover your sleuth skills

Your everyday behaviors can give you hints about what skill might set you apart from other people.

If you answered mostly a's . . .

your special skill may be your attention to details or your interest in exploring and gathering information. You could be great at figuring out the clues in a case and determining the facts.

If you answered mostly b's . . .

your special skill may be seeing how the pieces fit together to solve a mystery, like a police detective or a field scientist would do. You may enjoy using a high-tech tool, whether it's a special microscope or the latest in spy gizmos.

If you answered mostly c's . . .

your special skill may be interviewing and understanding people. You may like figuring out how people think or why they act the way they do.

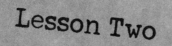

Lesson Two

On the Lookout

Do you pay close attention to what's happening in the world around you? It may take a little extra concentration to be sure that you don't miss anything!

Test your powers of observation.

Eye of the spy

How observant are you? Take some guesses right now about these things that are around you every day. Afterward, test your family, too. How observant are they?

1. How many windows are on the front of your house?

_____

2. Is there wallpaper in your parents' bathroom?

_____

3. What coffee mug is your mother most likely to drink out of?

_____

4. What color are the walls in your living room?

_____

5. Where do your old newspapers go until they can be recycled?

_____

6. How many kinds of salad dressing are in your refrigerator?

_____

7. What radio station will be on in the car when it is turned on?

_____

8. What is under your bed right now?

_____

9. Is there a cup on the bathroom counter? If so, what color is it?

_____

10. How many chairs are in your living room and kitchen combined?

_____

Scoring

9–10 correct: ## Eye-spy genius
What can we say? You're great at observing. Not much slips by without you noticing it.

6–8 correct: ## Eagle eye
You have an eye for the not-so-obvious. Keep practicing and pretty soon you'll
be amazing!

3–5 correct: ## Watchful eye
You're on the right track. Look around to see if there are other things you could
have noticed.

1–2 correct: ## Eye in training
Keep practicing. Some interesting things may be slipping past you. Try paying extra
attention for a couple of days and then take this quiz again.

Back-to-back quiz

Do you notice details about the people you hang around with?
Sit back-to-back with a friend. See if you can answer these questions about her correctly. Then give your friend the book and have her write *her* answers. No peeking!

1. Are her ears pierced? _____ _____
your answer   her answer

2. Is she wearing earrings today? _____ _____
your answer   her answer

3. Is she wearing a belt? _____ _____
your answer   her answer

4. What color is her shirt or blouse? _____ _____
your answer   her answer

5. Does she have a ring on her finger? _____ _____
your answer   her answer

6. On which side is her hair parted? _____ _____
your answer   her answer

7. Does her hairstyle have bangs? _____ _____
your answer   her answer

8. Is she wearing a necklace? _____ _____
your answer   her answer

9. What kind of shoes is she wearing? _____ _____
your answer   her answer

10. What color are her eyes? _____ _____
your answer   her answer

Scoring

9–10 correct:
Friends forever
Way to go! You noticed a lot of things that someone could easily miss.

6–8 correct:
Fine friends
Good job! You remembered a lot of details about your friend.

3–5 correct:
A friend indeed
You're well on your way to being an observant friend. Keep noticing the details about people around you.

1–2 correct:
A friendly start
Try this quiz again with someone else, to see how many more correct answers you can get. You'll probably notice more of the little things the next time around.

The suspicious case of the missing info

Are you the first one to notice when something is missing? Can you tell when things aren't quite right? Try these brainteasers.

Picture puzzle

Use your skills to detect what's missing in each picture:

1.

2.

3.

The answers are on page 59.

Puzzle pieces

Which piece would finish the jigsaw puzzle?

Word puzzle

What word is missing in each of these sentences?

1. Mary wondered which the dancers had left her slippers in the dressing room.

_____

2. The cat chased dog around the block.

_____

3. The kids all ran home when school let out 10 A.M.

_____

The answers are on pages 59–60.

Track 'em down!

Someone who solves mysteries needs to be able to find her way around. How good is your sense of direction?

Get the point

Stand outside facing the front door of your home. Follow these instructions, and then ask an adult to tell you if you did each one right:

Right **Wrong**

1. Point north.

2. Point in the direction of your school.

3. Point in the direction where the sun sets.

4. Facing away from your house, point in the direction of your best friend's house.

5. Close your eyes and turn in what you think are two complete circles. With your eyes closed, point in the direction of your front door.

Find the field

Solve the following maze. Get the girl from school to home to the soccer field without going off the track or hitting a dead end.

The answer is on page 60.

Take direction

Use the directions below to guide you along the map shown.
Where do you end up?

Leave Kim's house and walk EAST. At the end of the street, take a LEFT.

Go over the bridge. At the fork in the road, stay to the RIGHT.

Take the next RIGHT turn.

1. What is the second building on the EAST side of the street?

_____

Leave Carol's house and walk WEST.

At the end of the block, turn LEFT and walk two blocks.

Turn EAST, and walk to the end of the street.

Turn NORTH. At the fork in the road, stay to the RIGHT.

After you go under the railroad bridge, turn LEFT at the fork in the road.

Turn LEFT at the next street. After the library, turn LEFT again.

Take the first RIGHT, and stop at the first building on the RIGHT.

2. What building are you in front of? Did you take the shortest route to get there from Carol's?

_____

_____

The answers are on page 61.

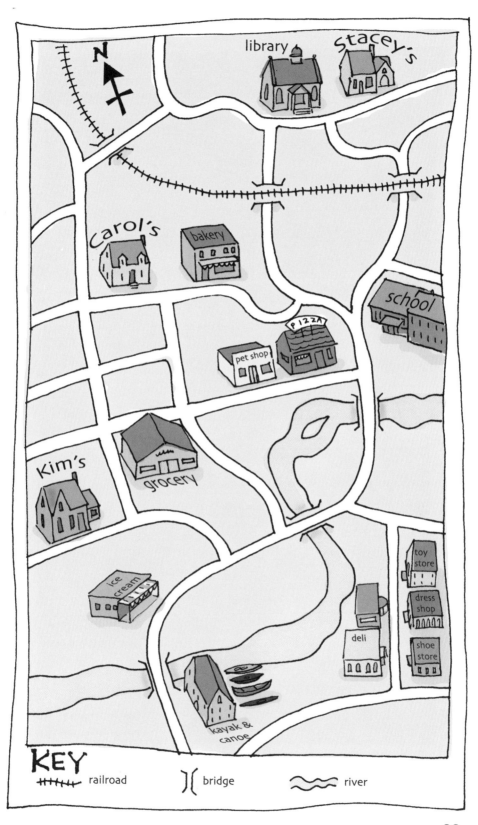

library

stacey's

Carol's

bakery

school

PIZZA

pet shop

Kim's

grocery

ice cream

toy store

dress shop

deli

shoe store

kayak & canoe

KEY

╫╫╫╫ railroad   ](bridge   ～～ river

23

Take a close look

A mystery fan needs to pay attention to all kinds of details. Read this paragraph and count all the o's as fast as you can.

One scientist wondered if studying for a test by reading the material over and over was the best way to remember it. She asked one set of volunteers to memorize a list of words by repeating them for three minutes. She asked another set to find as many ways as they could to put the words into groups (such as animals, names of cities, and so on). When she took the list away and asked the volunteers to recall the words, people who had organized their lists remembered many more words than people who simply repeated them. The scientist decided organizing and understanding material was a better way to study for a test.

How many o's were there?

_____.

Now count again. Did your answer change? If it was different, count again! The answer is on page 61.

Memory quizzes

A super sleuth needs to have a good memory to keep track of the details of a case. There are several types of memory skills you may be called on to use.

Your **short-term memory** helps you recall something you just saw, heard, touched, or tasted.

Your **incidental memory** helps you recall something you may have noticed but weren't trying to remember.

Your **long-term memory** helps you recall something you learned a long time ago.

Short-term memory test

How well do you remember something you just saw? Study this picture and try to remember all the items you see. Now turn the page.

Short-term memory test, part 2

Write down as many items from the picture as you can.

_____ _____ _____

_____ _____ _____

_____ _____ _____

_____ _____ _____

_____ _____ _____

_____ _____ _____

**Go back and check the picture. Give yourself
a point for every item you recalled.**

Points _____

Incidental memory test

Can you recall something you weren't actually trying to remember? In the drawing on the previous page there was a billboard in the background. Without turning back to look, answer the following questions.

1. What is being advertised on the billboard? _____

_____

2. What color is the animal shown? _____

3. What color is the animal's collar? _____

The answers are on page 61.

Long-term memory test

Can you remember something you learned long ago? Find out by answering the following questions. Check your answers afterward with a parent.

1. What was the name of your kindergarten teacher?

_____

2. What city did you live in when you were three years old?

_____

3. What was your favorite cartoon or television show to watch when you were little?

_____

More Super-Sleuth Skills

A super sleuth needs to have a questioning mind and keen eyes. Plus she needs to be prepared, persistent, and patient! You can get what it takes—just look, listen, and learn.

People profiles

Although every person is different, knowing how to *profile*—guess things about a person because they are often true of a group she belongs to—can help you figure things out about someone involved in a case. See if you can predict how **your friends** would answer the following questions. Then guess how **your parents' friends** would answer. Put "yes" or "no" in each box.

	My friends	My parents' friends
Would you like to own a pet hamster?		
Do you like staying up past 11:00 at night?		
Do you watch the news at least five times a week?		
Do you play on a sports team?		
Have you played hide-and-seek this year?		
Did you go grocery shopping in the past two weeks?		

How did you do?

Ask three people from each group for their answers. Did your profiling ring true most of the time? Sometimes you can make pretty good guesses based on, for instance, whether the person answering is a kid or an adult. Always be sure to check out your assumptions, however, because every person is unique.

Just the facts, ma'am

Answer these questions about your mother, father, grandparent, or another adult relative or friend. Check your answers with that person or with someone who knows him or her. You might hear some interesting stories!

1. In what town or city did this person go to grade school?

_____

2. What sport, if any, did this person play growing up?

_____

3. What is his or her phone number?

_____

4. Does this person have e-mail?

_____

5. To what magazines, if any, does this person subscribe?

_____

6. Has this person ever met a movie star? (Give yourself an extra point if you can say who it was.)

_____

7. Has this person ever been in a play?

_____

8. Has this person ever ridden a horse?

_____

Scoring

You may have heard some of the answers to these questions if you were paying close attention at family gatherings over the years. But some details you can learn only from asking people! Listening well and asking questions are important skills for anyone who loves mysteries.

7–8 correct: Great job!
You must have listened carefully in the past and asked some important questions. Kudos to you!

4–6 correct: Wow!
You know a lot of information about this person. Take the next opportunity you have to find out even more.

1–3 correct: Keep it up!
You already know a little about this person. If you ask more questions, you'll find out even more fun facts.

How high is your antenna?

Circle the letter next to the answer that best describes how you would act in each situation.

1. You walk into a party where all the people are talking to one another. You . . .

   a. go right to the refreshment table, barely looking at anyone.

   b. spot the first person you know and make a beeline for her.

   c. look around the room to see who else is there.

2. You arrive at a shopping mall with your friend. You . . .

   a. head straight for the store you've always shopped at before.

   b. ask your friend where she wants to go, and try that store first.

   c. wander around the mall to see what stores might have the best sales.

3. As you hurry between classes at school, you . . .

   a. focus on the papers in your hand all the way to your class.

   b. talk to the person you are with, noticing only the people who shout "Hi."

   c. watch everyone who goes by, checking out who's walking with whom.

4. While the teacher is lecturing in math class, you . . .

   a. focus on the numbers the teacher is writing on the board.

   b. catch yourself daydreaming but get back on track.

   c. watch the kids around you to see what they're doing. Hmm . . . what was the teacher saying?

Scoring

If you love solving mysteries, you need to pay attention to the details around you. But there can be a lot of distractions. Are you tuned in just enough, too much, or not enough?

If you answered mostly **a's . . .** you're like a **jogger wearing headphones.** You're listening to the one station that is tuned in. Having your mission firmly in mind probably helps you get things done, but you'll want to tune in to the outside world now and then, too, so that you don't miss something important.

If you answered mostly **b's . . .** you're like a **weather radar** system that is ready to detect an oncoming storm. You focus on what you're doing right now, but you're still alert and waiting for signs. Even so, you shouldn't always rely on someone else to make you take notice. Check your signal to be sure you're picking up everything you need to know about what's happening around you.

If you answered mostly **c's . . .** you're like a **radio tower.** Your antenna is super high, so you're bound to notice even the littlest thing that's happening. That's great, as long as you don't get distracted from what you are supposed to be doing. Be sure you are focusing on the task at hand. You wouldn't want to miss something that's right in front of you.

Got it? Check!

Grab your backpack and your purse. Between the two, how many of these items do you have? Check all the boxes that apply.

❑ A pencil or pen

❑ Paper to write on

❑ A paper with your name and phone number on it, to identify your bag if it is lost

❑ An eraser to correct errors

❑ A safety pin to fix a rip or a tear

❑ Tape to fix something or stick a note to someone's locker

❑ Your homework, finished or not

❑ A ruler to measure distance

❑ Your friends' phone numbers

❑ A snack to carry you over to the next meal

❑ A cloth or plastic bag to carry something in

❑ Keys to unlock your door

❑ Sunglasses, in case it is bright out or you need a disguise

❑ Postage stamps

❑ A flashlight

Scoring

A mystery solver needs to be prepared at all times. Are you ready for anything? Or are you carrying so much that you can't find what you need when you need it? Give yourself one point for each item you had in your bags.

9–15 points:
Overloaded
You tend to carry all kinds of things with you "just in case"—probably even things that you don't need. Are you stuffing your bags with supplies you'll never use? You might want to lighten your load.

5–8 points:
Ready as ever
You're rarely caught without something you need, and you probably tend to plan in advance. Since you're so well prepared, you may end up loaning things to classmates who aren't quite as organized as you are.

0–4 points:
Traveling light
You tend not to carry many supplies around with you. This might work fine if you have a friend who doesn't mind loaning you something. But it's better to plan for yourself and carry the things you need most often, in case your friend is not there to help out.

Eye for adventure

See how ready you are for adventure. Choose the answer that best describes what you'd do in each situation.

1. You get a chance to take a raft trip down the Colorado River! You . . .

   a. go by yourself, even though you don't know anyone else on the trip.

   b. find someone who went before so that you can ask how her trip was.

   c. say "No way am I getting in a raft!"

2. You're wearing your grubbiest clothes. It's raining outside. You're with a bunch of friends and there's a huge mud pit at the bottom of a steep hill. It's your big chance to get mucky! You . . .

   a. yell "Me first!" and jump right in.

   b. watch to see if others will jump in first.

   c. imagine all the things that could happen, and decide not to slide in the muck.

3. It's snowing like crazy, and school is closed for the day. You decide to . . .

   a. call a friend and make a snowman in your front yard.

   b. watch a good movie on TV that you have seen three times before.

   c. stare out the window, daydreaming about how high the snow could get.

4. You come home from school to find that a pipe has broken and water is rushing into your basement. You . . .

   a. grab some of your parents' tools and look for the water shutoff valve.

   b. call someone to help you start bailing the water.

   c. sit down for a minute and think about all the different things you could do.

Scoring

Solving mysteries is not always for the faint of heart! Certain cases may require a taste for adventure. Do you prefer to be in the action, or do you like a mystery that can be solved from the comfort of your kitchen table?

If you answered mostly a's . . .

you're ready for adventure and probably prefer a mystery that takes a lot of action to solve. Have fun moving and grooving on the way to a solution!

If you answered mostly b's . . .

you're likely to take action when it's needed but might not be the first to get your hands dirty.

If you answered mostly c's . . .

you may enjoy mysteries that require thought or research rather than getting out in the field to find the answers.

The stakeout

As a detective, you could be called on to watch all night for a suspect to come out of a building. What do your everyday behaviors say about how well you would do in this situation? Choose the answers that best describe what you'd do.

1. When your older sister asks you to watch the cake she's baking, you're most likely to . . .

    a. turn on the light in the oven and peek in regularly.

    b. turn the temperature up a little higher to get the cake done quickly.

    c. check your e-mail, call a friend, and read a magazine in between cake checks.

2. While knitting a scarf, you discover that you dropped a stitch several inches back and a loop is hanging out. You're likely to . . .

    a. rip back as far as needed to pick up the stitch, and keep knitting until your scarf's long enough.

    b. pull the whole scarf off the needles and start knitting a different project.

    c. find something else to do. You might come back and fix the scarf later.

3. You're at a meeting about the school play and you have to go to the bathroom, badly. You . . .

    a. wait till the meeting ends, even though you're miserable.

    b. scoot out of the room immediately, no matter what you'll miss.

    c. giggle with a friend to distract yourself as long as possible.

4. You stay up late studying, and the next day you have to watch a boring movie in class. You are most likely to . . .

a. stare at the screen as long as you can, then lay your head down on the desk.

b. fidget around, picking up a pen that you keep dropping.

c. doodle on your notebook, glancing up to watch the movie.

5. You're sitting on your bed, reading a book that you just bought for fun. You . . .

a. read it cover to cover because you're so lost in the story.

b. hop up several times—to get a drink, find a pillow, and get more comfortable.

c. read the same paragraph three times because your favorite songs keep coming on the radio.

6. When you're making a scrapbook with a friend, you . . .

a. find all the pictures of the two of you together, cut them out one by one, and keep going until you get the whole scrapbook done.

b. stop each time you look at a new picture to talk with your friend about what happened that day.

c. get distracted looking at pictures from other scrapbooks you've done.

7. You find a robin's nest in a tree, and it has baby birds in it! You wonder where the mother is, so you . . .

a. watch the nest carefully until the mother bird flies back.

b. check all the trees and bushes to see if you can find the mother.

c. watch for a while, run into the house to find something you can do while you're waiting, and stop to call a friend while you're inside.

Scoring
The Stakeout

Sometimes it can take all night to catch a suspect. And you need to watch, wait, and pay close attention. How might you do at a stakeout?

If you answered mostly a's . . .

you're likely to be patient and able to wait. To stay alert, think about what you might do if the suspect runs to the right or the left. Or count the bricks around the door of the building to keep your eyes on the target.

If you answered mostly b's . . .

you're pretty aware of anything that moves. But staying in the car on a stakeout could be your biggest problem. If you jump out at the first person you see, you'll blow your cover.

If you answered mostly c's . . .

you probably can make the best of a boring situation, which is likely to help you stay awake on a long stakeout. Just be sure you don't get too distracted or you could miss the suspect when she comes out.

Operation Brainstorm

To solve a mystery you need to know how to make a hypothesis, an educated guess based on the facts and details that you observe.

How do you start? By learning to brainstorm a number of possible answers to a question and then figuring out which one makes the most sense.

Possibilities

Guess again!

When working on an investigation, a super sleuth will look for facts and make educated guesses to answer the questions in the case. Make your best guesses about the following. Afterward, verify the real answers and see how close you were.

If I had to guess . . .   Points:

. . . how many pages are in my town's
  phone book,

I'd say: _____

The real answer is: _____   _____

Within 100 pages = 1 point
Within 50 pages = 2 points

. . . the temperature outside right now,

I'd say: _____

The real answer is: _____   _____

Within 20 degrees = 1 point
Within 5 degrees = 2 points

. . . the time right now, to the minute,

I'd say: _____

The real answer is: _____   _____

Within 15 minutes = 1 point
Within 5 minutes = 2 points

. . . of the next four people I ask, how many would say they like dogs more than cats,

I'd say: _____

The real answer is: _____

———————————
1 number off = 1 point
Exact guess = 2 points

TOTAL POINTS:_____

Scoring

Using what you know to make an educated guess, rather than a wild one, can get you closer to solving a mystery every time.

6–8 points: Right on

You have an amazing ability to guess the right answers, probably because you're thinking about all the things you already know about a given situation. For example, in figuring out the temperature, you may have thought, *It's after noon, the sun is out, and it's warm for the season.* Don't be fooled, though. You'll still want to test out your guesses.

3–5 points: Close call

You made some great educated guesses! Thinking through what you know about a situation can help you deduce the things you *don't* know. Narrowing down the answer is what an investigation is all about.

0–2 points: Keep guessing

Don't worry; some things just aren't obvious. Guessing correctly depends a lot on knowing other things about a situation. For example, in figuring out what time it is, it helps to remember what time it was when you last checked. The more data you can gather, the easier it is to guess correctly. Keep checking out those facts.

Take a hint

Have you ever noticed something unusual and wondered what might have caused it? If you find yourself daydreaming about logical reasons for unlikely occurrences, you may have what it takes to be a detective or scientist.

What might have caused the following situations? Give as many answers as you can in the left column. In the right column, name something you could check to learn whether or not your answer is correct. Turn to pages 46–47 to see if you came up with some of the same ideas we did.

You find a large broken branch in the woods.

What could have caused this:	What I'd need to check to be sure:
1.	
2.	
3.	
4.	
5.	

You touch the front of a car and notice that it is warm.

What could have caused this:	What I'd need to check to be sure:
1.	
2.	
3.	
4.	
5.	

There is a cup of very cold water on your kitchen counter, but no one is home.

What could have caused this:	What I'd need to check to be sure:
1.	
2.	
3.	
4.	
5.	

You find a large broken branch in the woods.

	What could have caused this:	What I'd need to check to be sure:
1.	A big animal passed by and stepped on it.	Are there animal tracks around?
2.	A person broke it on purpose to point the way.	Are any twigs stripped of leaves, suggesting that a person did it?
3.	A deer was eating the branch.	Are there teeth marks?
4.	The branch was rotten and fell down.	Is the inside of the branch soft and rotten?
5.	A strong wind blew the branch down.	Are other branches or trees down?
6.	A bulldozer broke off the branch.	Are there bulldozers or bulldozer tracks around anywhere?

You touch the front of a car and notice that it is warm.

	What could have caused this:	What I'd need to check to be sure:
1.	Someone drove the car recently.	Is the engine itself warm under the hood?
2.	The car was on fire.	Are there puffs of smoke or flames? Do you smell smoke?
3.	The car is warm from the sun.	Is it sunny? Are other parts of the car warm?
4.	A person was just sitting on the hood.	What is the shape of the warm spot?
5.	Your parent set a hot casserole on the hood a moment ago.	Is there a casserole around anywhere? Do you smell food?

There is a cup of very cold water on your kitchen counter, but no one is home.

	What could have caused this:	What I'd need to check to be sure:
1.	The air in the room is very cold.	Is the air-conditioning on high? If it's winter, is a door open?
2.	Ice cubes in the glass melted just recently.	Are ice cubes missing from the tray in the freezer?
3.	Someone left the cup there recently.	Did someone just go out the back door?
4.	The whole cup of water was frozen, but it just finished melting.	Are there other cups of frozen water in the freezer?

Scoring

How many ideas did you come up with?

7 or more ideas: Clue master

You did a great job coming up with lots of ideas. You may have even more theories up your sleeve! Developing a habit of noticing the small details and thinking of all sorts of solutions could make you a fine detective.

4–6 ideas: Quick thinker

You've thought of many different ways that things could have happened. Stay curious about the world. Ask yourself questions and think of many possible answers. They're the first steps in any investigation.

1–3 ideas: Strong starter

You've made a great start! Most situations have several possible explanations, if you stop to think about them. Look for the not-so-obvious in a variety of settings. How did that piece of paper get in your yard? What made that tree grow a certain direction? With a little practice, you'll come up with all kinds of possibilities.

Think up a storm

How many possible solutions can you list for each situation below? Even silly answers are important—they can sometimes lead you to other, useful ideas. *Remember, not all ideas are safe, so you wouldn't want to try them.* Our answer list is on page 50. If you come up with ideas we didn't think of, write and let us know!

1. You're lost in the woods and need to get across a river. How might you do it?

2. Name as many ways as you can to use a paper clip.

_____

_____

_____

_____

_____

_____

_____

_____

3. The zipper on your backpack breaks and your stuff is hanging out all over. What could you do?

_____

_____

_____

_____

_____

_____

_____

Possible solutions

To cross the river:

- Check to see if the water is shallow enough to wade across.
- Knock a tree across the water and crawl over.
- Walk upon large stones that are in the water.
- Swim across.
- Walk upstream to see if the river narrows. Cross there.
- Call for a boat to take you over.
- Use the canoe you are carrying.
- Blow up plastic bags and use them as flotation devices.

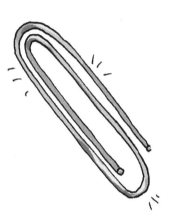

Uses for a paper clip:

- Hold papers together with it.
- Hook something onto your backpack with it.
- Get more paper clips and make a chain.
- Get even more and make a belt.
- Scratch your back with it.
- Use it to lock or unlock your luggage.
- Twist a bag shut with it.
- Use it to clean out a pen that's clogged with dried ink.
- Dig a hole with it.

To deal with a broken backpack zipper:

- Spread out the teeth on each side of the zipper, and push the sides together to see if you can fix it.
- Tape it with duct tape.
- Pin it with safety pins.
- Put everything in the backpack inside a plastic bag, and wrap it shut with a rubber band.
- Tie a rope around the whole thing.
- Put the things that are falling out into a friend's backpack.
- Buy a new backpack.
- Borrow a backpack that works.
- Carry a gym bag instead.

Lesson Five

Exercise Your Mystery Muscles

Keep your skills sharp by solving even more brain-busters!

Mind-benders

Quick scramble

How many new words can you make out of the letters in these words?

1. BINOCULARS

2. SCIENCE

_____ _____ _____ _____

_____ _____ _____ _____

_____ _____ _____ _____

_____ _____ _____ _____

_____ _____ _____ _____

_____ _____ _____ _____

_____ _____ _____ _____

_____ _____ _____ _____

Unscramble

Unscramble these words, and then read the sentence they make. Could this be a clue?

Uoy ear a sprue shutle.

_____

Answers are on page 61.

Get the picture?

Sometimes what you see is not what it seems to be. Suppose you saw the following images through your telescope. Guess what each one could be.

1.

2.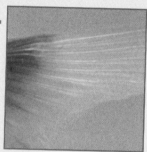

3.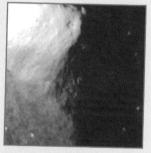

4.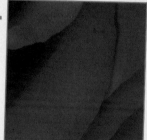

5.

6.

Answers are on page 62.

A few favorite things

Are there simple things you don't know about the folks you thought you knew best? In the blanks, write the favorites of people you are close to. Afterward, check your answers with them.

	Person #1	Person #2
1. Favorite color	_____	_____
2. Best friend	_____	_____
3. Favorite sport to play	_____	_____
4. Favorite sport to watch	_____	_____
5. Favorite subject in school	_____	_____
6. Favorite movie star	_____	_____
7. Favorite song	_____	_____
8. Favorite hobby	_____	_____
9. Favorite magazine	_____	_____
10. Favorite candy	_____	_____

Scoring

How did you do?

8–10 correct:
Wow!
You're a top-notch information gatherer. Check often to learn if this person's favorite things change.

5–7 correct:
Good job
To know so many things about this person, you must talk to her a lot.

0–4 correct:
Keep at it
People change their preferences all the time, so now that you've discovered this person's favorites, check back now and then to stay in the know.

Code-name creator

Detectives sometimes use code names to hide their identities or codes to communicate secret information. To come up with your exotic code name, look up the letters in your name on the code key below.

A = I	H = R	O = A	V = Z
B = C	I = Y	P = W	W = J
C = T	J = B	Q = X	X = Q
D = G	K = V	R = H	Y = U
E = O	L = K	S = F	Z = D
F = N	M = L	T = S	
G = P	N = M	U = E	

Sample code names:

KATIE = VISYO
JESSICA = BOFFYTI

RACHEL = HITROK
EMILY = OLYKU

Write your name and your friends' names here:

_____ = _____
first name   code name

_____ = _____
first name   code name

_____ = _____
first name   code name

_____ = _____
first name   code name

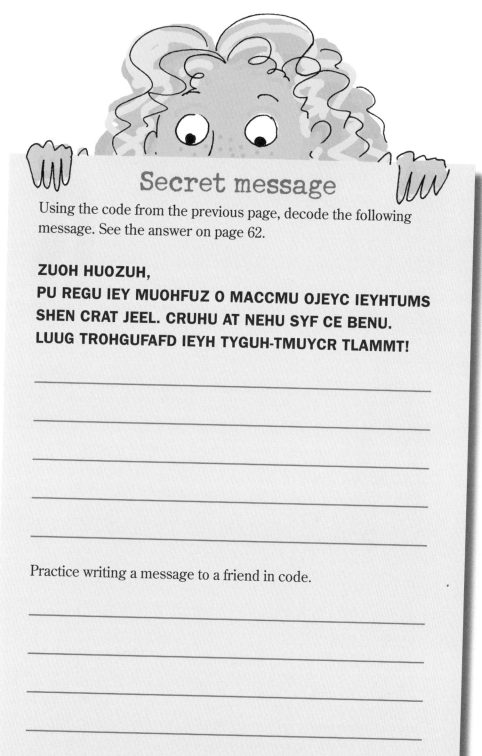

Secret message

Using the code from the previous page, decode the following message. See the answer on page 62.

ZUOH HUOZUH,
PU REGU IEY MUOHFUZ O MACCMU OJEYC IEYHTUMS
SHEN CRAT JEEL. CRUHU AT NEHU SYF CE BENU.
LUUG TROHGUFAFD IEYH TYGUH-TMUYCR TLAMMT!

_____

_____

_____

_____

_____

Practice writing a message to a friend in code.

_____

_____

_____

_____

Congratulations!

Whether you choose to be a scientist, investigator, private eye, detective, or something else entirely, your sleuthing skills can come in handy. Being smart, curious, and observant can help you whether you become a teacher, an artist, an engineer, or a newspaper reporter—to name just a few other careers.

You don't have to decide right now what you want to do in the future. Just stay curious about everything around you. There's a world full of mysteries—and adventures—out there waiting for you!

Super-Sleuth Degree

This hereby certifies that

_____

has successfully completed

The
I L♥ve Mysteries
Fun Book

Answers

Picture puzzle page 18

1. One flower doesn't have a stem.

2. A finger is missing from one of the gloves.

3. One of the chairs has only three legs.

Puzzle pieces page 19

Piece **C** is the missing piece.

Word puzzle page 19

1. Mary wondered which **of** the dancers had left her slippers in the dressing room.

2. The cat chased **the** dog around the block. (The words **a, our,** or **my** would also work.)

3. The kids all ran home when school let out **at** 10 A.M.

Find the field page 21

Take direction page 22

1. The dress shop

2. You're in front of the bakery. You definitely didn't take the shortest route to get there!

Take a close look page 24

There are 39 o's.

Incidental memory test page 26

1. Arlo, the dancing dog

2. Arlo is golden brown.

3. He's wearing a red collar.

Quick scramble page 52

1. Some of the words found in *binoculars*: acorn, ails, also, barn, bin, brain, cabins, can, club, in, irons, is, lab, lair, lion, nail, no, nor, oil, or, our, rail, rain, robin, sailor, soar, sun, uncoil, urn, us

2. Some of the words found in *science*: in, is, ice, ices, nice, niece, nieces, scene, scenic, see, seen, since

Unscramble page 52

You are a super sleuth.

Get the picture? page 53

1. A violin

2. A goldfish

3. An apple

4. A rose

5. A globe

6. A clock

Secret message page 57

Dear reader,
We hope you learned a little about yourself from this book. There is more fun to come. Keep sharpening your super-sleuth skills!

What was your favorite part of
The I L♥ve Mysteries Fun Book?
Write and tell us at:

I L♥ve Mysteries Editor
American Girl
8400 Fairway Place
Middleton, WI 53562

(All comments and suggestions received by American Girl
may be used without compensation or acknowledgment.)

Here are some other American Girl books you might like:

❏ I read it.

❏ I read it.

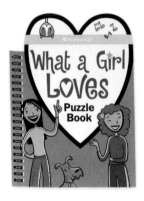

❏ I read it.

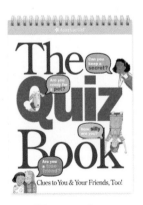

❏ I read it.

❏ I read it.

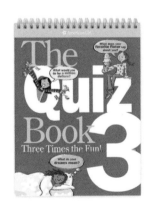

❏ I read it.